COLOUR ME MINI BEASTS

Buster Books

T0118916

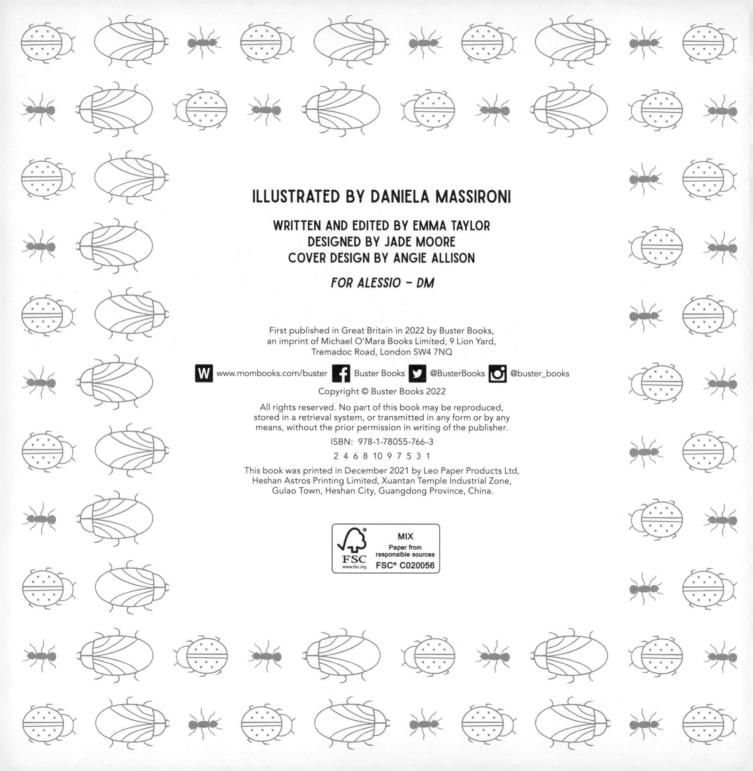

ILLUSTRATED BY DANIELA MASSIRONI

WRITTEN AND EDITED BY EMMA TAYLOR
DESIGNED BY JADE MOORE
COVER DESIGN BY ANGIE ALLISON

FOR ALESSIO – DM

First published in Great Britain in 2022 by Buster Books,
an imprint of Michael O'Mara Books Limited, 9 Lion Yard,
Tremadoc Road, London SW4 7NQ

W www.mombooks.com/buster f Buster Books 🐦 @BusterBooks 📷 @buster_books

Copyright © Buster Books 2022

All rights reserved. No part of this book may be reproduced,
stored in a retrieval system, or transmitted in any form or by any
means, without the prior permission in writing of the publisher.

ISBN: 978-1-78055-766-3

2 4 6 8 10 9 7 5 3 1

This book was printed in December 2021 by Leo Paper Products Ltd,
Heshan Astros Printing Limited, Xuantan Temple Industrial Zone,
Gulao Town, Heshan City, Guangdong Province, China.

FSC
www.fsc.org

MIX
Paper from
responsible sources
FSC® C020056

ABOUT THIS BOOK

This book is packed with all of your favourite mini beasts, from brilliant beetles and bumblebees to colourful caterpillars and butterflies. Next to each picture is a fun fact to discover as you colour.

Sometimes this book will tell you what colour the insects are, but if you want to colour all of them in exactly the right colours, why not use their names to look them up on the internet? Otherwise, you can colour the bugs in this book in any colours you like.

So grab your pens and pencils and get colouring!

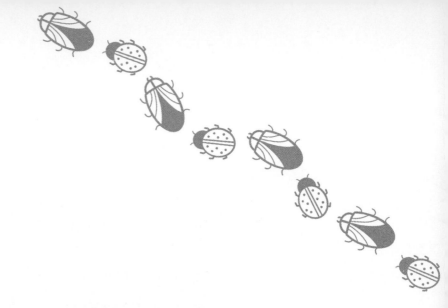

STAG BEETLE

This insect gets its name from the jaws on top of its head,
which look a lot like the antlers on a stag. Only male stag beetles
have very large jaws. They use these jaws to wrestle
other males when trying to attract a female.

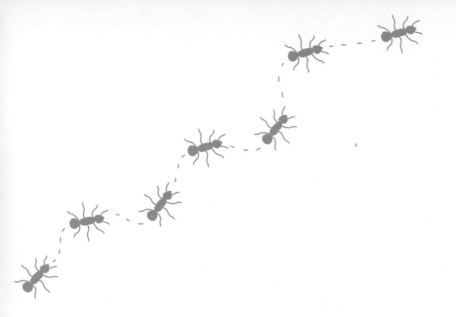

FIREFLY

Fireflies are nocturnal, which means they only come out at night. They have special body parts that glow in the dark, which they use to communicate and to attract a mate. Sometimes, a large group of fireflies come together and flash their lights at the same time.

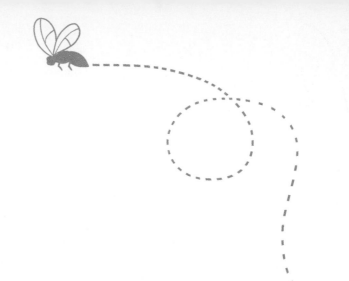

RED ADMIRAL BUTTERFLY

This butterfly has velvety black wings, red stripes and white speckles.
It can be found across the Americas, Europe and Asia, from gardens
and seashores to the tops of the highest mountains.

SNAIL

Snails have spiral-shaped shells on their backs, which they use to hide in when they sense danger. They come in lots of different sizes. The giant African snail can grow up to 30 centimetres (12 inches) long, which is about the same length as a guinea pig.

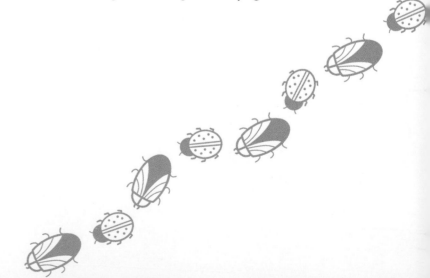

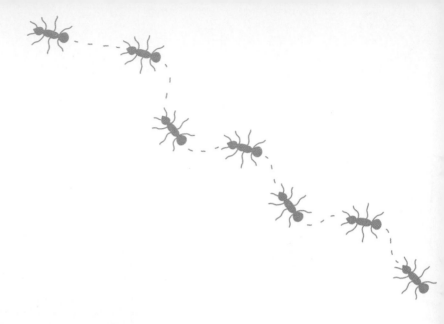

CICADA

A cicada is a flying insect that makes a very loud buzzing or clicking noise. There are different types of cicadas and some make more noise than others. The loudest can be almost 120 decibels, which is as loud as a clap of thunder.

GRASSHOPPER

Grasshoppers have powerful back legs used for jumping.
Some grasshoppers can jump 20 times the length of their own bodies,
which is the same as an adult human jumping the length
of a football pitch in three leaps.

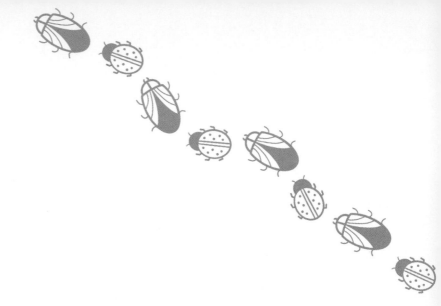

EMPEROR DRAGONFLY

Emperor dragonflies are one of the biggest and fastest types of dragonfly found in Europe. They have large wings and bristly front legs, which help them to catch their prey while in the air. Male emperor dragonflies are blue and females are green.

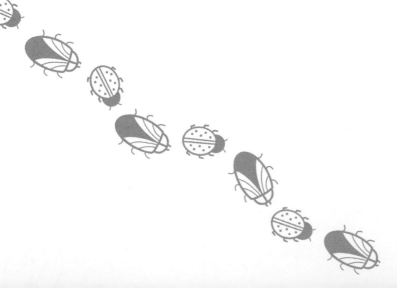

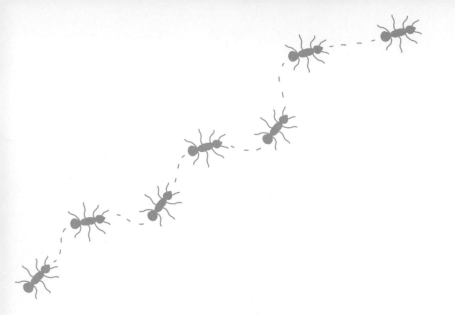

BULLET ANT

This ant can be found in the tropical rainforests of Central and South America. It is named after its incredibly powerful sting, which is said to be the most painful sting of any insect.

MADAGASCAN
SUNSET MOTH

This colourful moth can only be seen in Madagascar, an island
off the coast of East Africa. It has blue, green and red markings
on its wings, which warn predators that it is poisonous.

HONEYBEE

Honeybees carry pollen between the male and female parts of flowering plants, helping them to grow seeds and fruits. They can fly as fast as a running bull and beat their wings 200 times per second.

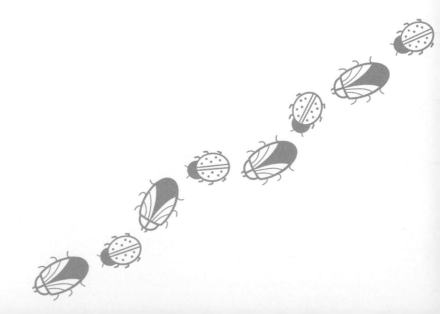

CALLETA SILKMOTH CATERPILLAR

These colourful caterpillars have turquoise or orange studs
that are tipped with black spines. This helps to protect them from
predators – no one wants a spiky snack!

FLOWER CRAB SPIDER

Just like a crab, this spider crawls sideways.
It can change the colour of its body to match its surroundings
and hide from its prey. It likes to eat insects that feed on
nectar, such as honeybees and butterflies.

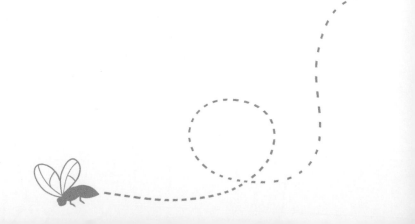

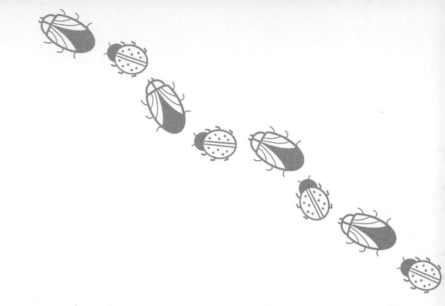

CENTIPEDE

This creepy-crawly has a long body and many pairs of legs, which it uses to scurry after its prey. The Amazonian giant centipede from South America can grow up to 30 centimetres (12 inches) long and eats small animals such as mice and bats.

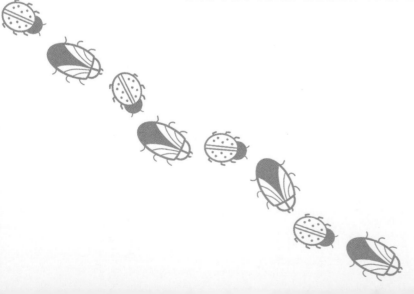

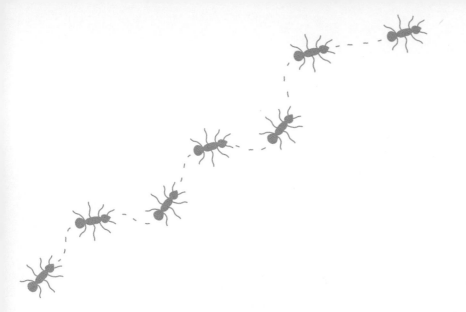

DID YOU KNOW?

Beetles make up over a third of all insect species.
There are over 380,000 known types of beetle in the
world, with many still yet to be discovered.

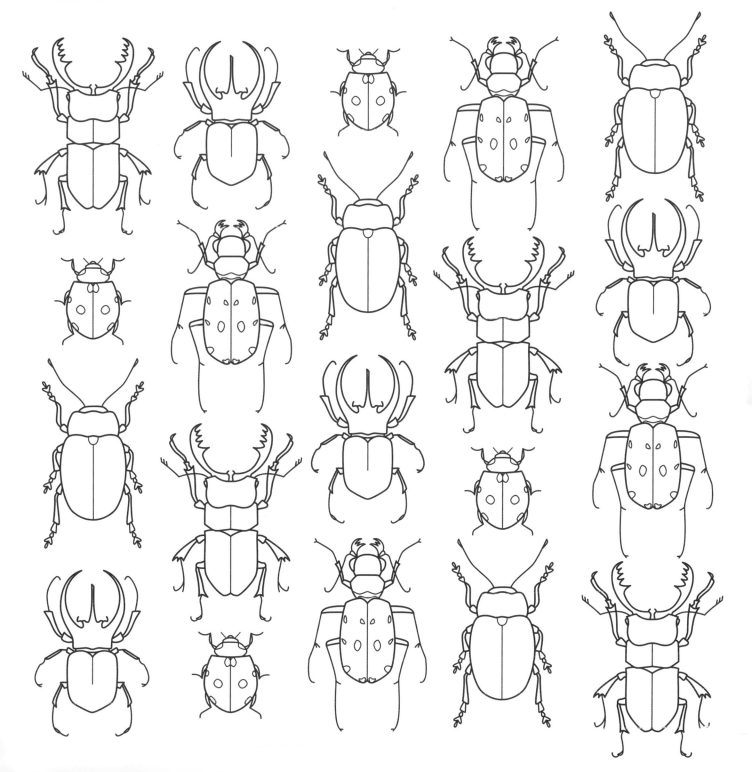

PRAYING MANTIS

This critter is a fearsome predator that can catch and kill its food at lightning speed. It is green or brown in colour, which helps it to blend in with its surroundings and hide from its prey.

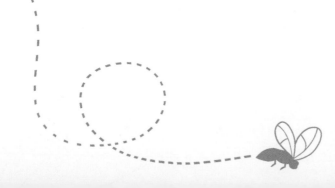

QUEEN ALEXANDRA'S BIRDWING

This colossal insect is the largest butterfly in the world, with a wingspan of 28 centimetres (11 inches). Males have emerald-green wings with black stripes, while the females' wings are brown and marked with white spots.

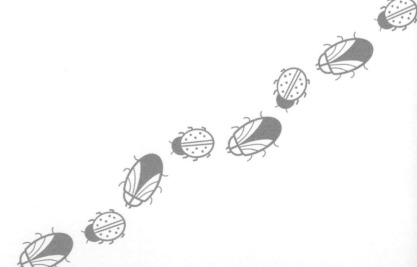

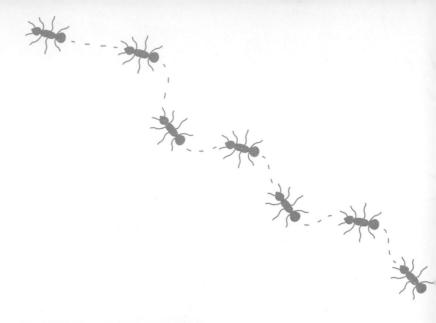

WOODLOUSE

These mini beasts can be found sheltering in cool, damp places such as compost heaps and under logs. Female woodlice have a pouch under their bodies, similar to kangaroos, where they lay their eggs.

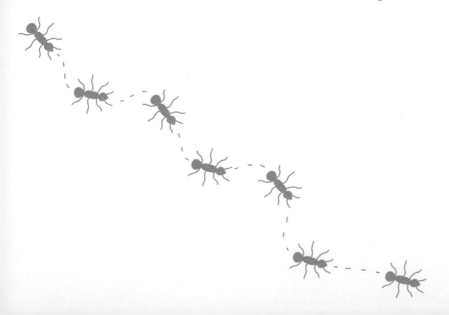

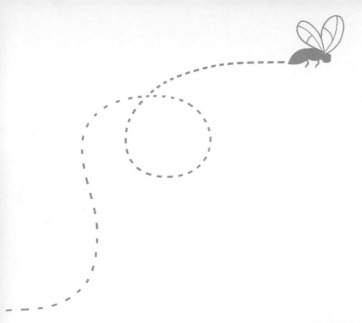

LADYBIRD

Most ladybirds have brightly coloured bodies with black spots.
Their markings stop them from being eaten by other animals as they make
the ladybirds look poisonous. These bugs love to eat small insects called
aphids and can gobble more than 5,000 of them in a single year.

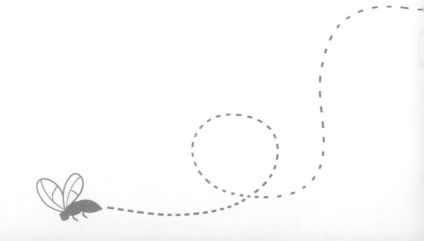

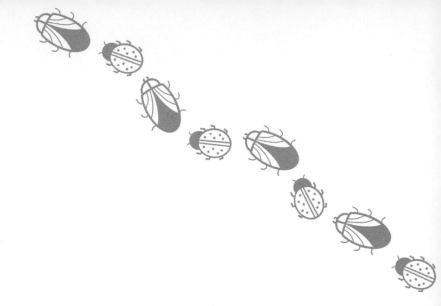

GOLIATH BEETLE

This beetle is one of the biggest beetles on the planet and can grow up to 11 centimetres (4 inches) long. It is also very strong and able to lift a load around 850 times heavier than its own weight.

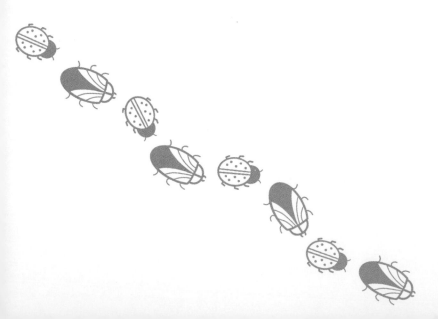

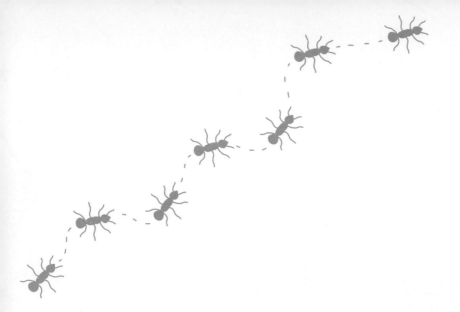

LEAF INSECT

Leaf insects have round, flat bodies and are green and brown in colour. This helps them to blend into their surroundings and hide from predators. Their camouflage is so good that sometimes they mistake one another for food!

EARTHWORM

The body of an earthworm is made up of ring-like parts covered in lots of tiny bristles, which help it to move along the soil and burrow underground. Most earthworms are small in size, but some can grow up to 35 centimetres (14 inches) long. That's the same length as a small snake.

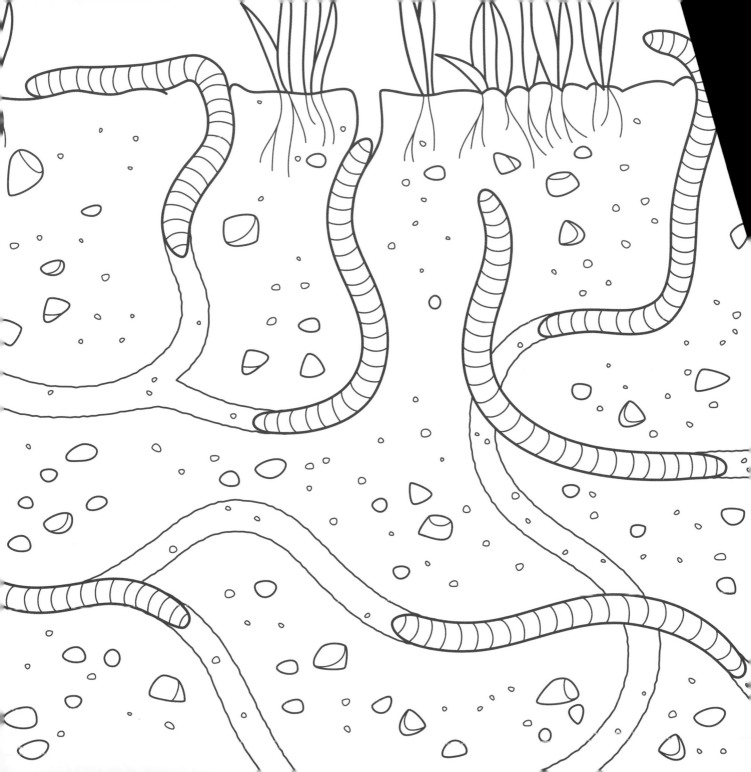

SLUG

Slugs have no skeleton at all. To get around, they produce
a slippery slime from their bodies, which allows them to slide along
the ground or climb up surfaces, such as garden pots.

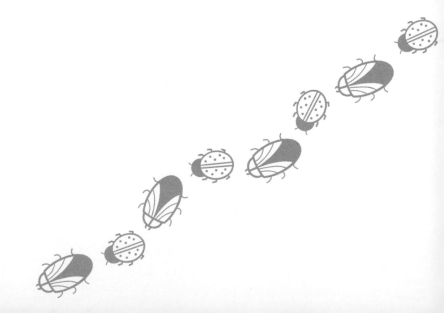

SWALLOWTAIL BUTTERFLY

This colourful butterfly gets its name from its forked tail,
like that of the swallow bird. It has two red-and-blue spots
on its tail, which look like eyes and confuse predators
into thinking that it has two heads.

WHITE-TAILED BUMBLEBEE

This bumblebee is black and yellow, with a bright white tail.
Like other types of bee, it sleeps (or 'hibernates') during
the winter and comes out in the springtime.

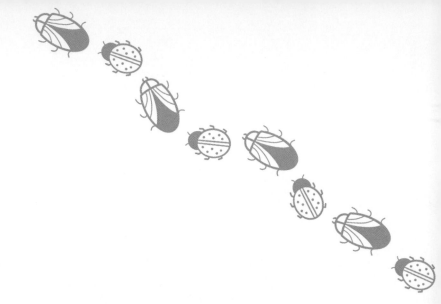

DUNG BEETLE

This small but mighty creature is said to be the world's strongest insect. When moving a ball of dung, it can push and pull a whopping 1,141 times its own body weight.

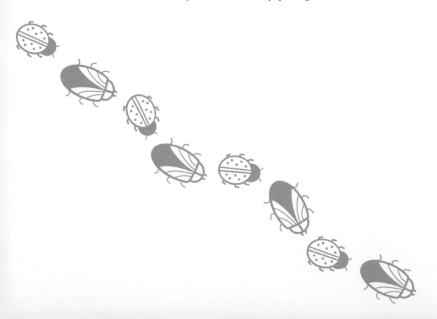

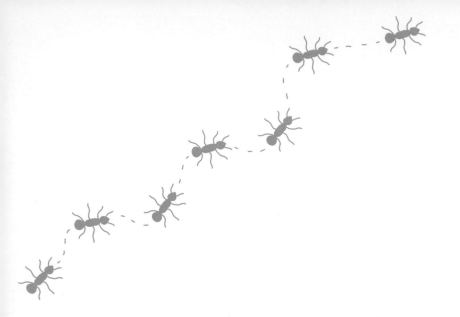

BLUEBOTTLE FLY

This noisy fly has a shiny blue body with black markings.
It belongs to the blow fly family, which contains over
1,200 different types of fly.

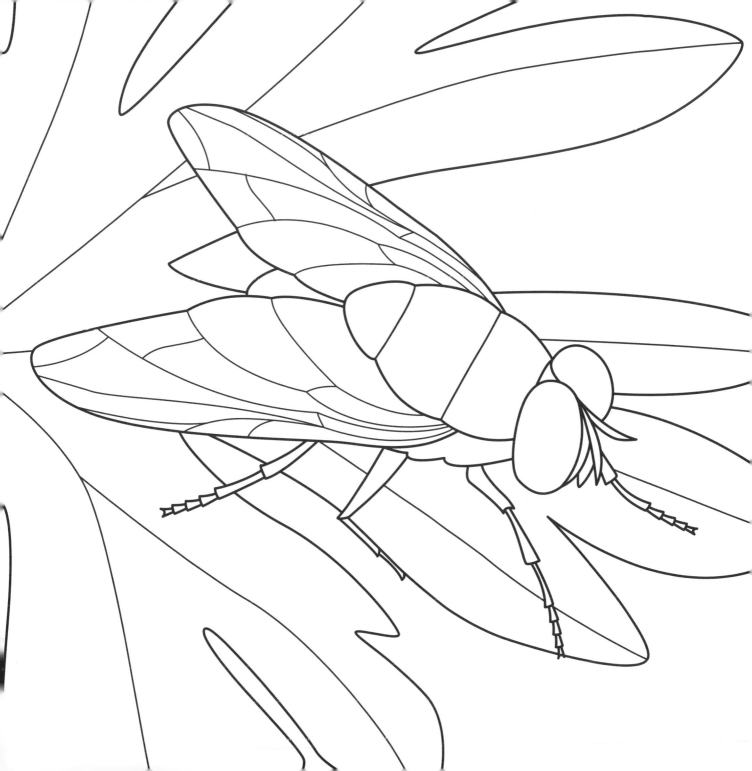

TREEHOPPER

Treehoppers have a sharp, pointed spike on their back.
This makes them look like the thorn on a plant and helps them to
hide from predators. To feed, they poke holes in the branches
of trees and suck up a sugary liquid called sap.

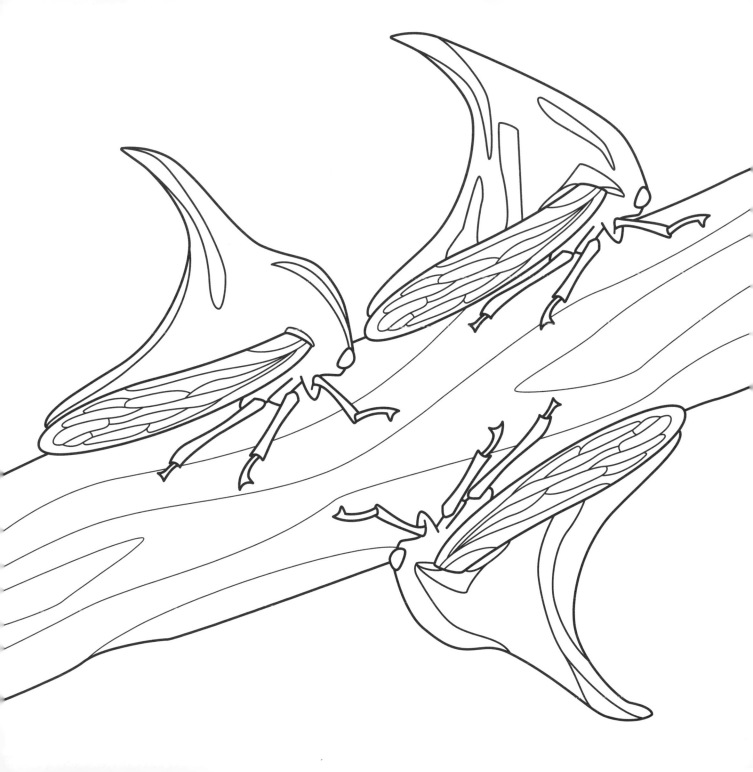

ATLAS MOTH

This gentle giant is one of the biggest insects in the world, with a wingspan that can stretch up to 27 centimetres (11 inches) wide. That's wider than an adult human's hand.

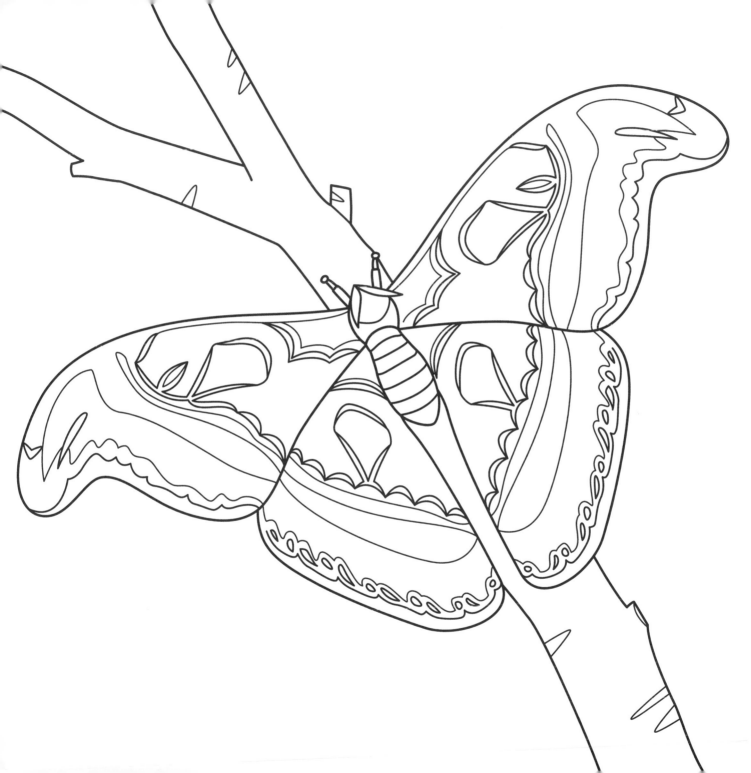

MADAGASCAR HISSING COCKROACH

This cockroach can make a loud hiss like a snake, which it uses to scare off predators. It is one of the largest types of cockroach in the world and can grow up to 10 centimetres (4 inches) long. That's almost as big as a house mouse.

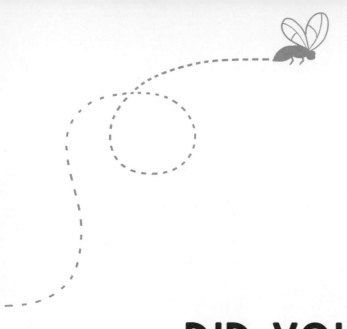

DID YOU KNOW?

Spider silk is incredibly strong stuff. Some scientists say that it is five times stronger than steel, making it one of the strongest materials known to man.

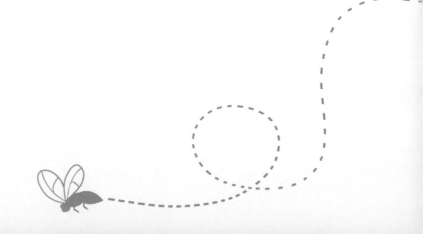

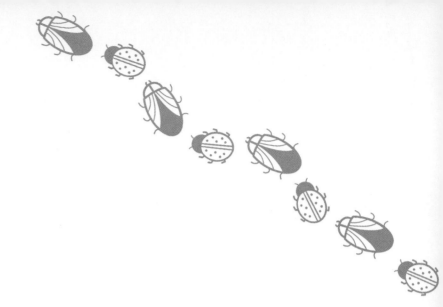

PICASSO BUG

The Picasso bug is no bigger than the size of
a small fingernail. It has a colourful, patterned body
with green, red, blue and black markings.

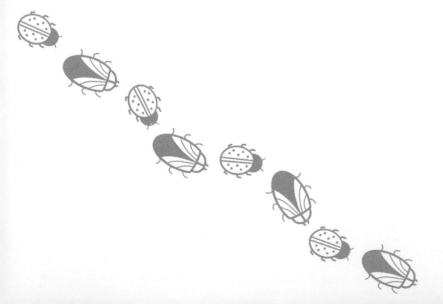

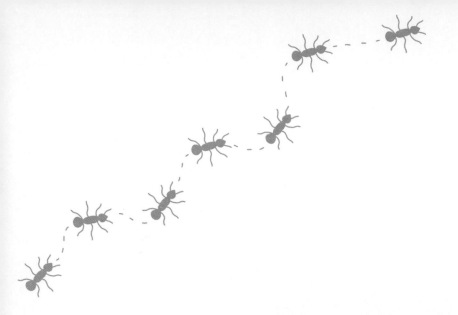

DAMSELFLY

Damselflies have long, slender bodies that help them
to balance while flying. They aren't as strong fliers as dragonflies,
but they have extra-large eyes for spotting their prey.

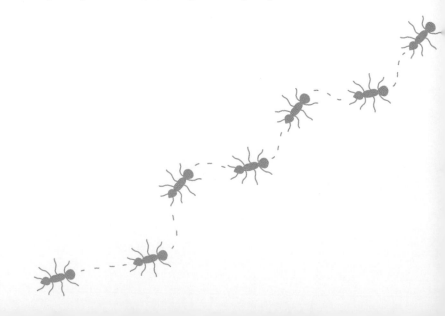

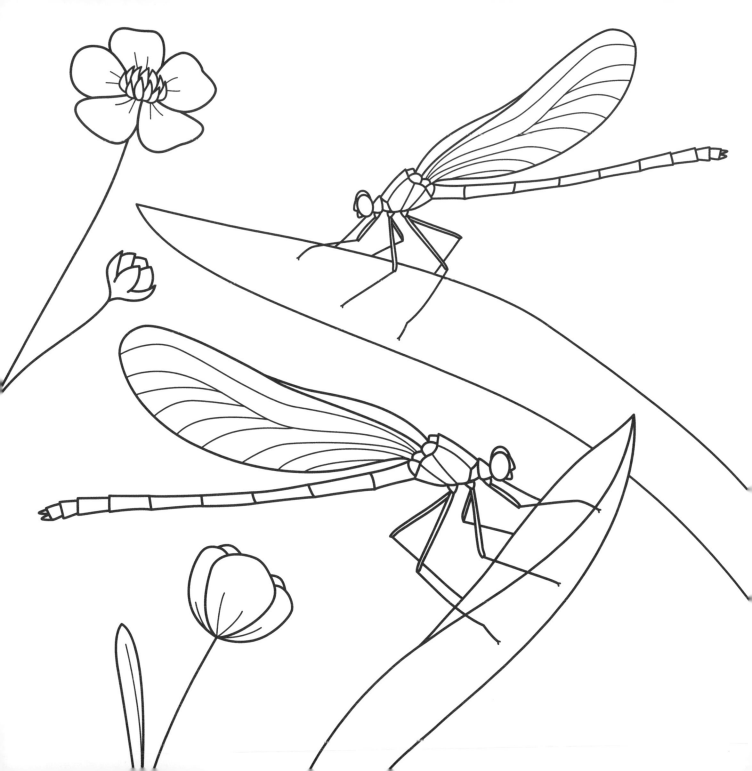

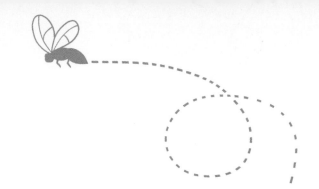

ORB WEAVER SPIDER

Orb weaver spiders build webs in the shape of a
circle and cover them in a sticky type of silk to catch their prey.
Some species can make webs that are over 1 metre (3 feet) wide,
which is the same length as a baseball bat.

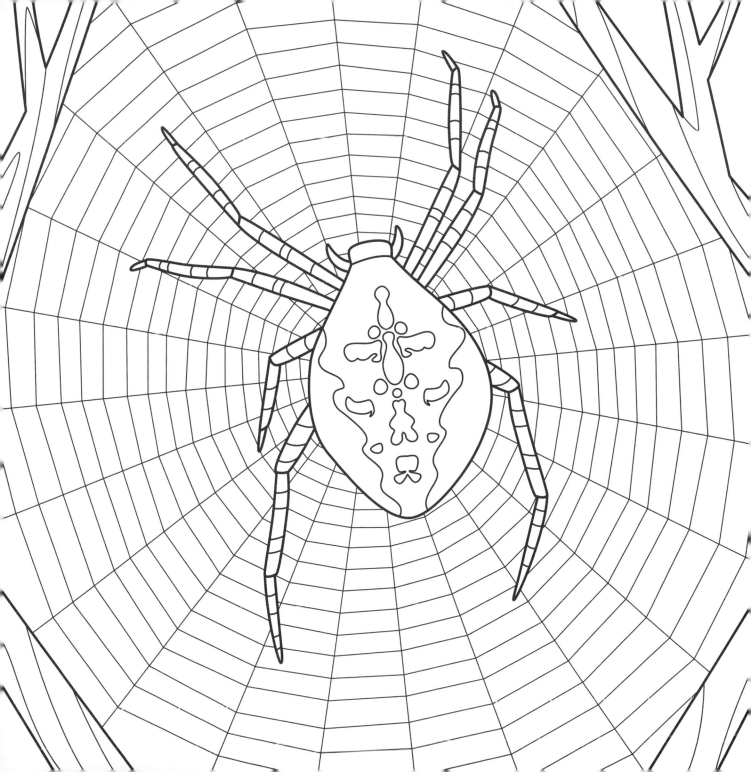

RHINOCEROS BEETLE

This beetle gets its name from the horn on top of the males' head, which looks a lot like the horn on a rhinoceros. It's nocturnal, which means it only comes out at night. During the day, it can be found sleeping under logs or hidden in plants.

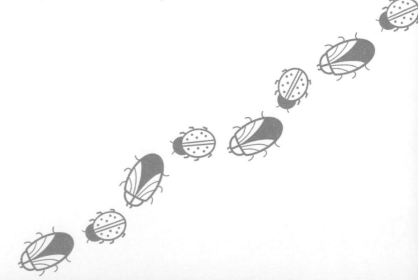

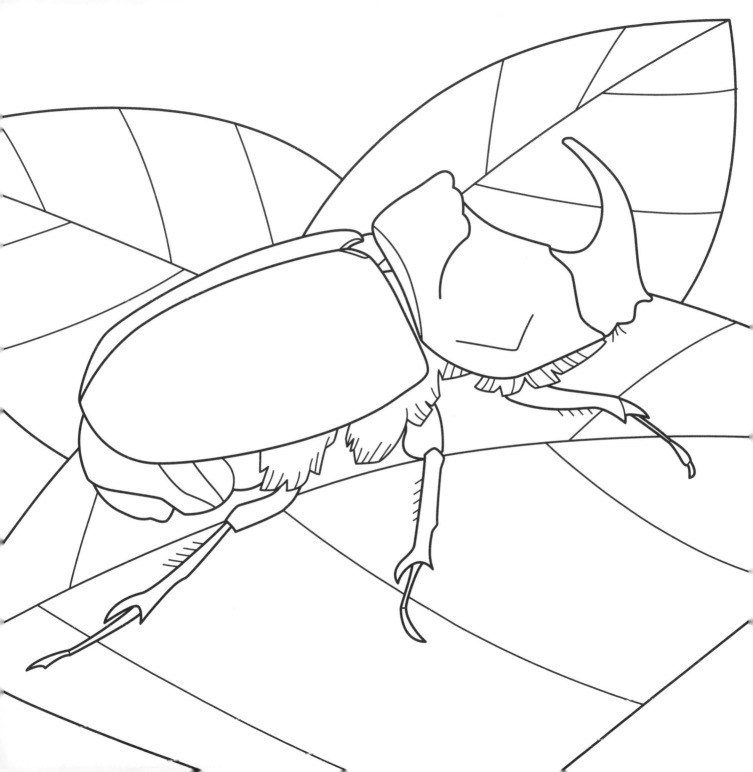

WASP

Wasps come in lots of different colours, from yellow to brown and blue to red. These bright colours act as a warning to predators that they are dangerous. Most female wasps have a stinger which, unlike a bee, it can use more than once to protect itself.

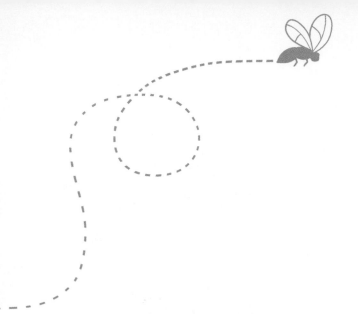

HICKORY HORNED DEVIL

This fierce-looking caterpillar is named after the black-tipped spines on the top of its head, which look a lot like horns. Most hickory horned devils are orange, blue and green.

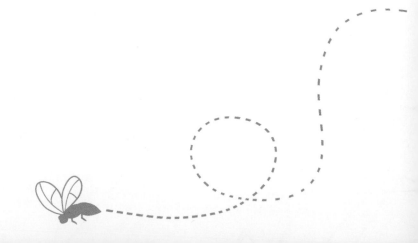

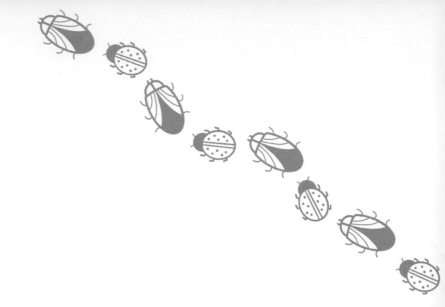

ORCHID MANTIS

Orchid mantises are some of the best masters of disguise
in the animal kingdom. Their bodies look like flowers called
orchids and some mantises can even change their colour
to blend in with their surroundings.

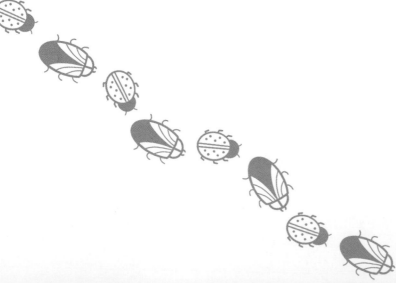

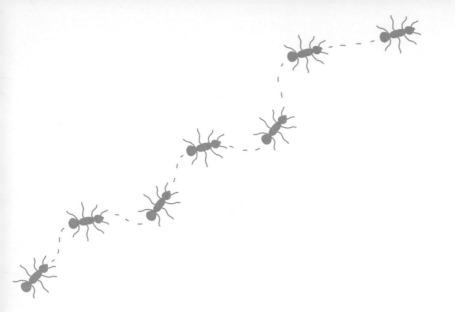

ROSE CHAFER BEETLE

This flying beetle is bright emerald green. It loves sunshine and can be found feeding on flowers — especially roses — during the summertime.

SCORPION FLY

Named after its scorpion-like tail, this fly is black and yellow.
It has a long mouth that looks like the beak of a bird, which it uses to feed.

SPOTTED LANTERNFLY

This jumping bug has two pairs of wings,
one that's grey with black spots and another that's red
with black spots. Although lanternflies can fly, they prefer
to hop and use their wings to help them.

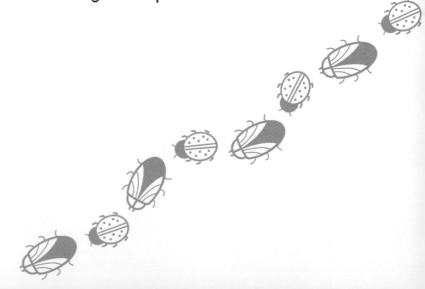

COTTON HARLEQUINN BUG

This colourful bug is a member of the jewel bug family, named for their bright metallic colouring. Females are mostly orange, while the males are mostly blue and red.

RED SPOTTED
JEWEL BEETLE

This beautiful beetle can be found on the coasts of Western Australia.
It has a green, shimmery-looking body with six red spots.

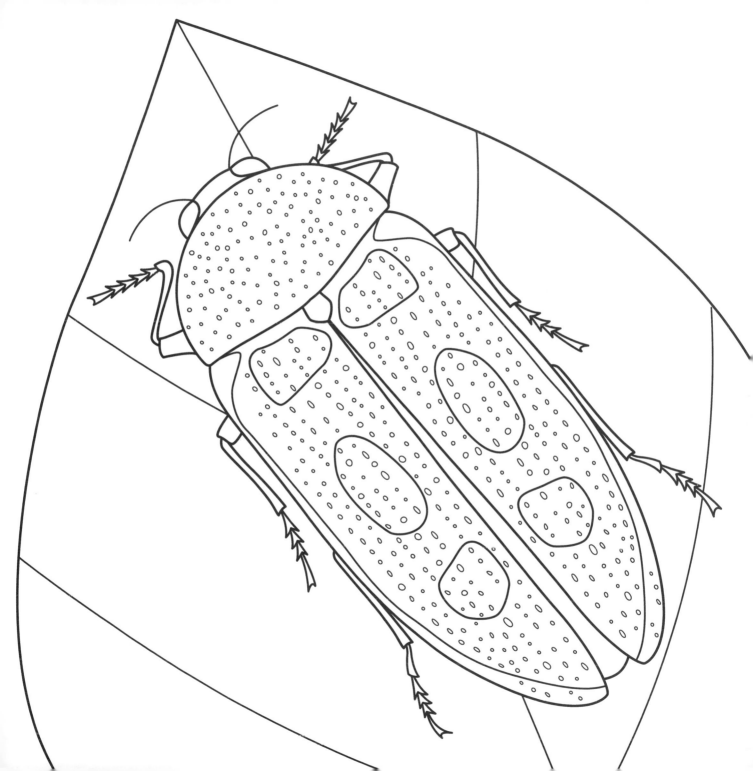

HUMMINGBIRD HAWKMOTH

This expert hoverer gets its name because it looks
like a hummingbird when it flies. It has grey, feathery-looking
wings and a long, thin mouthpart, which it uses to feed.
Its wings beat so quickly that they make a humming sound.

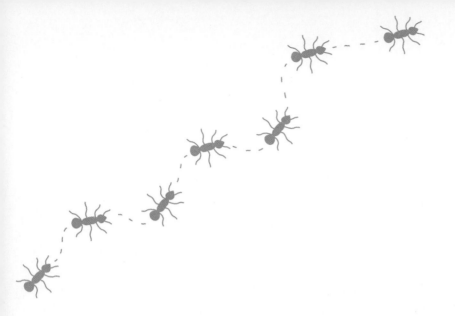

DEVIL'S COACH HORSE

This beetle comes out after dark to hunt its prey and uses
its pincer-like jaws to crush it. It is fast-moving and curls up its tail
when it feels threatened, much like a scorpion.

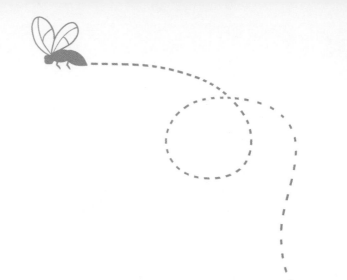

OWL BUTTERFLY

With spots on its wings that look like the eyes of an owl,
this spectacular creature can fool other animals into thinking
it's a bird. This helps the butterfly to scare off any predators.

PEACOCK SPIDER

Despite its impressive, colourful body, this spider is
no bigger than a pencil eraser. Male spiders' bodies can be
a mix of orange, blue, red and green.

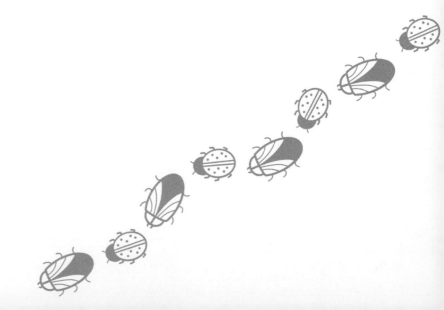